CARVER SCOTT

Tales of an African American Missionary

Part 1: Fundraising

Phoenix Enix Press

First published by Phoenix Enix Press 2025

First edition

ISBN: 978-0-9996009-2-4

This book was professionally typeset on Reedsy.
Find out more at reedsy.com

Contents

Introduction

I want to first thank you for your interest in this book. Whether you are reading it because you have close ties to me or you are just someone who wants to support the work that black missionaries do, it is appreciated. If you came across this book because it was recommended to you or you have some interest in the information it holds, I am thankful for you as well. My prayer is that you can gain something from what is written here. First and foremost, it is meant to be a resource for those who find or will find themselves in similar situations that I have faced as an African American missionary. I know that having this knowledge ahead of time could have helped me avoid some unfortunate circumstances. I could have advanced my ministry more effectively, and the momentum I built up would have continued without as many bumps in the road. This book is also for supporters of those who are African American missionaries who come from an African American church context. I want you all to have an insight into what is needed from people back home so that those in the field can have a more impactful ministry. Many times because of our history in the African American church, we have a viewpoint that is limited simply because long-term international missions have not been a significant part of what we do. However when God sends one of His workers out from among us, it is important to have an understanding of what is needed from the Body of

Christ to support the call of God.

The idea to write this book came about some time ago in my early years of living full-time outside of my native country. I had already gone through a time where I could see that a traditional missionary path, that being international work through missions organizations, was not suitable for me. At the same time, I did not encounter any resources that would point me in the right direction. Any book that I read regarding the task of fundraising for missions would speak to situations or resources that I just did not have. If there was any relevant information, it would be relegated to a page or two among 200 or so pages. Upon coming to this realization, it was evident that this road was not designed for people in my shoes.

While I would not call myself an expert in this area, I can say that I am seasoned in this field. I am still in the midst of my international work for the Lord, and in a number of ways, I am still finding what works best for me at different stages. As I write this, I have come off of eight years serving the Lord in Uruguay and will be transitioning soon to continue more work in Spain. As life evolves, one must also evolve with it. However, I do feel that I have a special insight that will be of help to those of my diaspora that are planning to live a life of international missions. The contents of this book will also help those who are going to be the support beams that hold missionaries up while they are abroad. I have seen that there is a lack of knowledge among our people in this area, and that is something that I want to rectify as best I can.

The topic of this book is based on my experience and what I have learned in my time thus far. My experience may differ from another person's, and it is not universal. I am an unmarried African American man, but things could be different for married couples or even a single African American woman. The situation could bring different factors if there is an interracial couple going to the field as there are two cultures potentially at play. It can change with age, if there are children involved, and many other factors. While my desire is to be of assistance to all of these groups, my experience comes mainly from the road I have walked and the testimony of those I have encountered along the way.

In this book, there will be certain terminology that will be used, and in this section, I will clarify their meaning so that we can have fluid and cohesive communication between author and reader. This book is speaking to the experience of the African American missionary. In this context, that specifically means people of the African diaspora who have the majority of their known history connected to the United States of America. To not be so wordy, from here on out, I will refer to those in this category as black instead of the longer term "African American."

Another term I want to clarify is the word "missionary." While some, especially in black churches, use the term "missions" to talk about doing a special project in the city or nearby, or even in a foreign land for a shorter trip, in this book, I will be using the term to describe those who are picking up their life to serve the Lord in a foreign land on a long-term basis. It is someone who leaves their current, native context and goes with a specific purpose in mind to build the kingdom of God. Anytime "missionary" is used in this book, it will be referring to foreign missions, rather than local missions unless otherwise stated.

Lastly, while this book may appear to do so at times, it is not meant to discredit mission organizations and how they have been utilized and implemented throughout our history. Rather, this book is meant to provide tools, ideas, and alternative solutions for the situation in which other black missionaries and I find ourselves. I recognize that black missionaries are a small demographic, and perhaps, you don't even know anyone who belongs to this group. However, my prayer is that this will change in the coming years as our call as followers of Christ is to share the gospel with the entirety of the world. Some are called to stay where they have always been while others have a call to stretch out to unknown lands.

I

What is a Black Missionary?

Chapter 1: Missionary

We will start by addressing the question in the title of this section. First, we must go back and ask, "What is a missionary?" Webster's dictionary simply states that it is "a person undertaking a mission and especially a religious mission." If I had to put a simple definition to it, I would simply state that it is a worker of the Lord who has been sent to a land outside of their native context in order to build the Kingdom of God in that area. Both of these definitions rightfully exclude the mention of any specific job being done because the reality is that the work of a missionary can extend to many areas. Generally when people think of mission efforts, they imagine going to some small village and building homes for the people. Others think that they are going to feed the homeless in an impoverished area. Very rarely do they consider that marriage counseling can also be a part of missionary work. Discipling can be a part of mission work. Helping a church's music ministry can be a part of mission work. Evangelizing to the public can be mission work. Having weekly games on a beach can be a part of mission work. It never has to look the same because the Body of Christ is diverse, and God wants to use the diverse gifts and talents of His people to reach the masses with His word. At the end of the day, mission work has the purpose of filling the spiritual needs that people have across the globe.

It is true that mission work often addresses a tangible need. It is hard to tell someone that they need to repent and turn to Christ if the sun is setting and all they have had to eat that day was a small bag of chips. It is hard to receive someone in your home if your home is made of cardboard. How can someone read a pamphlet given to them if they haven't had access to education that has given them literacy?

There is a story of a pastor who was going out in an area of the city with his crew to feed those who lived on the streets. They were giving out food from the back of their vehicle to those who had lined up. Among those receiving food was a big guy who looked intimidating upon first view. After getting his food, he went up to the pastor and shook his hand. While doing so, he looked firmly in his eyes and asked, "Do you have anything else for me?" He asked this while still holding firmly onto the pastor's hand. Noting the man's grip and the firm look into his eyes, the pastor started to think, "we only planned to give out one serving to each person, but maybe I should give this guy another so there won't be any problems." So he looked to his crew to see if there was any more food they could give to him. As they were getting it ready for him, the guy is still holding the pastor's hand. As the others are about to give him more food, the man says again to the pastor, "Don't you have anything else for me?" And the pastor was starting to question what this man meant. The man from the street finally said, "man shall not live on bread alone but on every word that comes from the mouth of God." It was then that the pastor realized what the man was asking for, and even more so, it reminded the pastor why he was there in the first place. The crew's tangible action opened the door to fulfill this man's spiritual needs also. His physical needs were met, but beyond that, he recognized that there was something more that he needed in his life. The food would be a temporary benefit to him, but what was most valuable was the door that was opened up for him to find the path to eternal life.

While this story was one pathway used to open the door to the gospel, it is not the only way. 1 Corinthians 9:19-23 says,

"(19) Though I am free and belong to no one, I have made myself a slave to everyone, to win as many as possible. (20) To the Jews I became like a Jew, to win the Jews. To those under the law I became like one under the law (though I myself am not under the law), so as to win those under the law. (21) To those not having the law I became like one not having the law (though I am not free from God's law but am under Christ's law), so as to win those not having the law. (22) To the weak I became weak, to win the weak. I have become all things to all people so that by all possible means I might save some. (23) I do all this for the sake of the gospel, that I may share in its blessings."

Some people are missionaries to give mental health counseling. Other people are looking to witness to nonbelievers in the musical performance world. Others are able to get with a group of bikers and relate to them. Still others can have a simple exchange because they are interested in anime culture. The point is to find the bridge that will be an area of connection so that Christ can be shared. Missionaries are those that use these bridges to "become all things so that they might win some for Christ" in a part of the world where they are not a native.

"Sometimes, you have to find a bridge. Other times, you have to

build a bridge. And then other times, you have to be the bridge"
-Carver Scott

Chapter 2: Black Missionary

Now that we have a general idea of what a missionary is, let's talk about what a black missionary is. I'll start with two key phrases that are very similar, but they will help you to understand what a black missionary is and what a black missionary lives. The first one is *"I'm a Christian first, but being black is a very close second."* The following one is *"I became a born again believer, but I was born black so I've been black all of my life."* These two thoughts are essential to understanding the dynamics that a black missionary has to live.

Being from the United States of America, race plays a large part in how we maneuver through society. While experiences vary greatly, there are common things that are shared throughout the core of the diaspora of African Americans. No matter your belief system, black people across the nation encounter many of the same experiences. This has been shaped by our shared history in the country, as well as the various sub-cultures of the African American diaspora. Behaviors such as greeting another black person you have never seen before just because you cross their paths is an example of one of these cultural characteristics that are shared. This is related to the part about "being black all of my life." It is something that I was born into, and because of where I grew up, it has been something that has shaped my way of life and understanding of the world. Those born under similar circumstances can relate.

Although I recognize the impact that my genes and my society have had on my life, my second birth is what has a greater weight on the way I live now. While there is no need to try to disconnect from my naturalized culture as a whole, there is no doubt that the newer life in Christ is what guides my movements inside and outside of the black context. The great thing about the Body of Christ is that it is diverse, and there is no need to say it has to be this way or that way exclusively. It is able to exist and permeate in all nations across the world.

It is important to note that not every aspect of every culture can coexist with Christianity. That is not what I am saying. Rather, things that are often seen as necessary to a "Christian/church life" are really just symptoms of traditions that have been shaped by a particular culture. Many would be shocked to see a pastor preach on Sunday without a suit or some kind of pastoral robes on. Upon searching for biblical examples of this particular custom, those same people may be surprised to find they have little support for the necessity of these garments.

I mention these things to help you realize that although I am black, being a Christian takes priority over anything in my life that might be a result of my blackness. Inversely, although I am a Christian, that does not mean that I negate the blackness that is an inseparable part of me, nor should I deny anything from that side of me that has shaped me into the person I am today. These two parts always coexist, and that is essential to keep in mind when considering the main theme of this particular book which is **fundraising for ongoing missionary endeavors as a black person**. Before we dive more deeply into that main theme, I want to talk a little bit more about what a black missionary lives because it leads us to why the support, both in prayer and in finances, is so important to have from those back home.

Chapter 3: Living as a Black Missionary

At its base, being a missionary means exchanging the life you have lived for a life that can be unfamiliar in many ways. This applies to missionaries of any ethnic background. We are going to a place where customs are different, people think and move in a different way, and many times there is the added layer of managing these differences in our non-native language. This alone can be an incredible weight to bear, and understandably, it is not a situation that all are equipped to live. Ideally, those who are on the mission field will not be there alone. Having connections with people who are native to the country as well as those who are foreigners with a similar goal helps to create a healthy balance in their lives. Even in cases where the connection with another missionary is not with someone from the same origin, there is a sense of understanding that is shared because both sides are experiencing this newer environment in a similar way and have to overcome similar obstacles with all of the changes involved.

During my 8 years of living in Uruguay, it was easy to see that most of my deepest relationships were not with the Uruguayan people. Instead, they were with those who were living in Uruguay as foreigners as well. This fact may be two-fold though. On one side, there is a connection with those other foreigners in our shared perspectives about certain "oddities" we saw in the Uruguayan way of living. The other part that may have influenced this is because I believe there is still the side of the Uruguayan people that does not permit meaningful relationships in the same way that relationships are created in many other cultures.

Focusing back on the church side of things, I'll share what happened in my experience. I lived in Uruguay from the ages of 30 to 38 as a single black man. I had different connections with white missionaries from the US. Many of them that were full-time, especially the ones 30 years old and above, were also married. Generally, the younger and unmarried ones that I met were in college or fresh out of college and were a part of a group in the country for a set amount of time, not necessarily on an indefinite basis like I was. I didn't have a core group present that I could relate to. Married people also have to be concerned about "married people" things. I was speaking to a missionary one time about some of the movements I made and what time of night I was active in certain areas of the city. He commented that he doesn't have the kind of freedom to be in those same places because he also has a wife and kids to take care of. His world looked a lot different than mine even though we were both on the same mission field. The stages of life we were in as well as our familial situations gave us different roads. To bring this example closer to home, mothers with small children are more likely to spend time with other mothers of small children as opposed to mothers without kids or with kids of a different age. This important area of their life allows them to share more in common with the other mother as well as give something for their kids to share.

Being a black missionary can be an isolating experience in many situations. In my particular case, I was living in a country that was largely of European ancestry, mostly Spanish and Italian. That is not to say that there are no remnants of the African diaspora there because there certainly are. In all of the countries of the Americas, we have an important presence, although some to a greater effect than others. However, in my initial description of what I mean by the term "black missionary," I specified that the term in this book pertains to those who have most of their known history connected to the United States. Black people are all over the world. Aside from Africa, there are those of the African diaspora that have their known history based in Latin America. Others are more closely tied to whatever European country they were born in, and still, others have lived their entire existence in places like Japan, all while sharing the physical characteristics of someone from the motherland. I mention this to again emphasize the role that culture plays in the shaping of our lives. I want to point out that culture often plays more heavily into how we relate than the hue of our skin.

Why is this important? Do you remember the example I gave of a black person greeting another person of their diaspora just because their paths crossed? This behavior doesn't really exist in Uruguay. While the lack of this was something I really had to get used to, it shows that I cannot connect with them in the same manner that I thought I could. That is one cultural difference, but we could assume that there are others as well. I say all of this to note that the experience is largely one where a missionary, and especially a black missionary, is in a very isolated space where the likelihood of finding someone who truly gets them is very low. If I want to connect with missionaries who are doing the same work as me, they can't fully understand my blackness. If I want to connect with the black native people who are in the country I am in, there will most likely be key cultural differences to where they won't get me. If there is a black person from the US in the country that I can get connected with, there is a probability that they don't have any, or have very little, connection to the faith that I have. Any shared experiences with any group is often incomplete as the pathway of a black missionary is uncommon to find.

This even extends to those back home. As a black missionary, many from the church don't understand why we would leave our homes behind and go to another land for the Lord's work. Some may even be intrigued and question the idea of a black man going to minister to a population that is largely white, such as in my case. "Christian first, black man second" was the idea I made sure to point out earlier. I want it to be clear that I am writing all of this to help bridge the gap between all of these areas, especially in the Christian world. I have seen that there are disconnects at different points in our understanding as the Body of Christ, and I want to help us all see what we can do to rectify these areas in order for us to stand more united. Understanding these matters gives us more unity, and in this case, helps us to make some important changes that are needed when it comes to raising funds for God's work as black missionaries.

II

How Did I Raise Funds?

Chapter 4: The Traditional Path

I want to start this section by explaining what my initial path was and then how I eventually came to finding what worked best for me. I mention again that everyone's journey may be different, but I believe that each black missionary can identify with a number of moments that I will mention in this section. If you are a black missionary who has yet to go out to your mission field, my prayer is that you will be able to maneuver these situations in a manner that helps to advance your calling rather than face obstacles without clear answers or tactics.

My first encounter with international missions came through an opportunity with a university group that took trips every two to three years. They would have some missionary connections in a country and would take a group to do outreach. The chosen country was different each time. It just so happened that while I was part of the group in 2011, the country chosen was a Spanish speaking one. I figured I could be of use since I majored in Spanish. This particular trip was a total of three weeks. Each person had to raise a certain amount of money, and we did so by tapping into our network. We did the normal solicitation route of telling our churches, friends, and relatives about what we wanted to do. People gave, and everyone that wanted to go was able to go. After spending these three weeks there, God placed it on my heart to go back again, and this time, I would go alone. I contacted the church family I had met while in Uruguay and began making arrangements to go back the following summer for a more extended time because I felt like the Lord had more work for me to do. Again, I raised the money that would be needed for the second endeavor. God provided temporary housing for me through the church I would be working with, and the work that the previous group had begun was able to continue through me. After the second trip to Uruguay, a similar thing happened, and I knew I would be going back again the following year.

By this time, people were getting more accustomed to my connection with Uruguay, and there was a pattern forming. From 2011 to 2013, I made three trips to Uruguay. With each year that passed, my stay extended a bit more. Obviously, I continued tapping in with those who were in my Christian network, and they were able to see more of what I was doing and how things evolved over the years. In those first years, there was no need to have ongoing support. I was following God's lead as He spoke to me. Therefore, each time that He said I needed to go back to Uruguay, I rounded up the troops and continued asking people to support me. The goal in those times was very current and in the moment. Up until that point I had made no official plans to move to Uruguay on a permanent basis.

After graduating with my Master of Divinity in 2014, I began to make more concrete plans to be in Uruguay full-time. I wouldn't just be there for two or three months, but I would be there living my life - spring, summer, fall, and winter. All seasons would be spent in this land where I was not born for the sake of building the kingdom of God. This is where my strategy for fundraising, and essentially surviving in this foreign land, needed to change. I needed to think about how to be able to live there on a long term basis. What I had done previously covered my needs for a few months, but this approach did not support a lifestyle.

I had gone to seminary because that was an example of what pastors had done to equip themselves better for their pastoral role. In the same way, I saw that missionaries who were in a full-time role were also a part of a mission organization. In my first years in Uruguay, I essentially was without an organization, and most of what I did was through God directing me and putting me with the right people. I saw the *result* of how mission organizations were used, and I figured it would be best for me to follow suit so that I could continue the work of the Lord in Uruguay on a more permanent basis.

Chapter 5: What Do Mission Organizations Do?

Before I continue recounting my journey, let's take a detour here and talk about what missions organizations actually do. We must keep in mind that parameters can vary from organization to organization. These are the main roles that I have seen mission organizations fulfill.

First, mission organizations give you a base of operations. Just like many local churches, mission organizations usually have particular areas of ministry that they focus on in their work. The one that I was a part of focused on Spanish speaking cultures, for example. Others have an emphasis on planting churches in areas that are needed. Another organization might be focused on sending out people who have skills in the medical field. Whatever their focus or aim might be, they are usually an entity that pushes a goal and helps to unite and send out those who will be in the field.

These organizations also help the missionaries to get set up in the country. Moving to a new country is a process with many steps, and after moving, there is still quite a bit that needs to be done to become established. If the missionary has little or no time that they have previously spent in the country, there will be a longer period of adaptation. This was not my particular situation as I had already spent a substantial amount of time in Uruguay before becoming part of a mission organization. I was already able to communicate in the language. I already had relationships with people that lived there. I didn't need much help in the matter of getting acclimated to a new setting. If you are a black missionary who chooses to do your work without a mission organization, it is a good idea to know as much about your country of ministry as possible. Know about your visas, customs, money, language, and more. This can be done on your own, but it is best to have someone alongside you to be of assistance on this journey. As I said, I already had a foundation in my country of ministry. If you do not, this is an important step in the process as well, and that is why mission organizations also provide help in this area.

Another role that these organizations fill is that of receiving the funds and helping them get distributed to each missionary. Things are made more official by having the name and brand of the mission organization so that people are not sending money to a person directly. Missions organizations also provide a sense of accountability with those on the field. Missionaries are under their banner and are also working for these organizations. Many, if not all, are expected to give regular reports about what is going on in the field. Some may even have certain quotas to meet for whatever kind of work is at hand. The missionary on the field is sort of an extension of that body so the idea is not to go out and disappear but to have continued contact with the head so to speak.

In my time of looking for a mission organization, I went to orientations for two different organizations. These are basically times in which you go to their headquarters, talk with the staff directly, get an idea of what they do as a whole and what their goals are, and see if you all are a good fit for each other. I ended up becoming part of an organization that I knew had missionaries that were already doing ministry with those I was connected to in Uruguay. I had three different trips under my belt by that point, and the idea was to carry the momentum in the relationships I had built previously. It was essential to continue traveling down a similar path rather than start a completely different journey in a place where I was already making my own lane. My ministry mostly dealt with building personal relationships with the people through whatever route I saw available. There was not much focus on meeting tangible needs. Rather, I saw I could help meet the spiritual needs of the people through real relationships so that I could show them the truth of the gospel. I will say that in whatever work you do, one of the primary factors to consider is to be with like-minded people. At a minimum, you should work with people that allow you to flourish in the areas in which you have gifts. Since I was trying to do things in a more official manner in Uruguay, I felt that this was an important requirement for the mission organization I would join.

When someone decides to join an organization like this, it is not as though they sign a contract one day, and then they are out in the mission field as soon as their bags are packed. Finding a mission agency is just the beginning step. From there begins what I would call the hardest part of the whole process, especially for a black missionary - fundraising.

Chapter 6: Successes and Failures with a Mission Organization

In my experience, missionaries are generally considered employees of their mission organization. I say this to the extent of having tax documents, W-2's, and all of that because of the work they do. What makes employment with these organizations unique is the fact that any money that is paid to the missionary is raised by each missionary or missionary family themselves. Therefore, there is an expedition to get enough funds to support the life that is going to be lived in this foreign country. Missionaries generally tap into their church and network of believers to help them reach their goal. What is very different here is that the goal is not to just raise a certain amount of money, $12,000 for example, and then you're ready to go. Instead, what the missionaries look for is monthly giving that will support the ongoing work that they will be doing. In the example of my first trips to Uruguay, there was a defined time period that I would be in the country. This helped me to aim toward a smaller goal. Being a full-time missionary is a different ballgame because generally, there is no end date. We are literally picking up our lives and saying, "Lord, I'm going to this place, and I'll be there until you move me somewhere else." It's a step of faith that typically does not have an end in sight.

Because of this, the support from the body of Christ needs to be different than it is for short-term missions.

The focus changes from a one-time event to an ongoing commitment. I say this in reference to both those who go and those who are sending out the missionary. Those that go to these foreign lands are committing their lives everyday to do what God has called them to do, and the goal is to have the church support them in this same manner on an ongoing basis. To make this practical, let us look at a clear example of the difficulties that can be faced in the process of raising funds to support a missionary.

To make the math easy, we will say that $12,000 per year is needed to live in this foreign land. Sure, a missionary could potentially get the funds for a whole year up front, but generally it would take longer to accumulate those funds. An easier path is to find people who are willing to give in smaller increments throughout the year. If you can find 10 people who are willing to commit to giving $100 a month to this missionary, that would cover all their costs for that year. If $100 a month is too big to ask of ten people, perhaps they could find 20 people who are willing to give $50 and that still covers the amount. Even 40 people who are willing to give $25 a month could be another alternative. Looking at these numbers on a smaller scale allows the goal to be more attainable. The idea behind getting these people to commit their giving in smaller increments does two things: 1) It makes the possibility of achieving your goal more likely and 2) it allows the missionary to get to their country quicker than they would if they had to have their full budget covered before they left. Once they know that they can pay for a place to stay, have transportation, and buy food, it allows them to move into their work more easily. However, this was the biggest hurdle that I found in trying to make it back to the mission field. After I finally settled on which organization I would be joining upon my return to Uruguay, it took me about two and a half years to finally be able to go. That is way too long, but allow me to explain what happened.

Mission organizations generally provide some kind of training on how to raise funds because it is such an essential part of being able to do the work. They provide resources and tools that help their missionaries find the people who will give, and they teach them how to sway potential supporters to be a part of the senders who will be giving toward their work in a committed fashion. There are books to read, and there are orientations and training sessions created for missionaries to attend. As I mentioned before, I've been black all my life. On top of that, I've been in the black church most of my life as well. As I continued to go through the readings and saw the tools they provided for us, it became more apparent that their strategies were not fitting in my cultural context.

It has been said that Sunday is the most segregated day in the United States of America, and that seemingly continues to be true even today. While there have been notable changes in recent years, it is still easy to see its prevalence. It is obvious that traditions and the history of our country have caused this particular area of our society to remain heavily segregated. Because of this, the customs that exist in these separate church cultures operate in a very different way. While the United States is a diverse country with many ethnic backgrounds, I will focus my comparisons mostly on the differences between white and black churches. There may be some similarities with Latin American churches or Asian American churches, but I do not have much experience within the United States in these areas.

My dealings have been mostly either with white churches or black churches in the US so I will keep the focus there.

I will give you all an example of one of the strategies that was given in order to help us missionaries be able to fund raise more effectively. I mention this one specifically because coming from my cultural context, this seemed like a ludicrous idea to me. It was particularly absurd to me because it was given as one of the first steps we needed to do in order to reach a "fully funded" status with the organization.

Getting supporters to join our team as monthly donors often includes the act of going to different churches and telling them about the missionary work that God has called us to do. The idea is that you would travel near and far to different congregations and essentially pitch your work to them. The expectation is that each missionary would be doing this in a fairly aggressive and full-time manner. They are to do this to the extent that having a regular job might get in the way. The thought is that if you put the work in now on the front side, you can get fully funded more quickly. Keep in mind that most people that go out are usually married at a minimum, and they might even have kids that are still living with them as well. There is more money that needs to be raised for each person added to the family unit. One of the reasons why I said my two and a half year period before being released into the mission field was way too long is because I am just a single person. If my memory serves me correctly, each missionary unit, family or single, was supposed to get their full funding within months by using this strategy that I am about to tell you all about.

So here is the route that was promoted by my mission organization at the time: They want each missionary unit to find people in their network who are willing to cover their living costs during the months prior to leaving for the mission field. The missionary unit would stop working any regular job so that they could dedicate their time fully to going to different congregations and groups in order to gather ongoing support for their mission efforts. An idea like this is completely unimaginable coming from my cultural context. I say it is absurd because it is a completely foreign concept to have a network of people who would be willing to pay for all of my costs of living so that I could raise funds. This is not to say that people I know would not be willing to help. Rather, it is a matter of wondering who in the world has that kind of economic status in my network to help sustain another person for that period of time. Even those who might have the economic status must also have the willingness to do so. The two parts need to go hand in hand, but that is a hard combination to find in my network. Let us note that at the time, my monthly expenses were not even close to some of those who were in orientations and training with me. I was just a single guy with an apartment, and I have always lived pretty humbly. Even with my relatively low cost of living, it was an impossible task to think I could even find one person who was willing to be part of that initial commitment.

I imagine that after reading the previous paragraph, there might be one of two reactions depending on your personal background. If you are similar to me, you might say, "Yeah, that's wild. I don't know anyone who might do that for me either. And if I do know a few who could give something in those months, it wouldn't be anywhere close to allowing me to quit my job so that I can focus on fundraising fully". If you are of a different background, you might have the thought of "Well, that is a big ask of someone, but I bet I could find a few people who might be convinced enough to go the extra mile for me for a few months."

I have never lived in abundance, and few people around me have lived in abundance so trying to get past step one of their process was already a failing point. Furthermore, at the time I was just barely getting by on my bills. I had to push many times to make sure all the bills were paid. I mention this again because any money that we had to spend for the task of raising funds came directly from the work of our own hand. For some orientations, we were expected to travel out of state. This means extra costs for airfare, hotels, and time off of work. For someone that was just making it by, this was another mandatory part of the process that caused me to be delayed in getting back to the land to which God had called me. They say being poor costs more than being rich, and this is a good example of it. If there is one extra cost in a month for something like having to fix your car or an unexpected medical expense, it's hard to recover after that because you are already just barely making it. Anything on top of that puts you in a deeper financial hole. Furthermore, my situation with the organization was a bit different because I wasn't even going to Uruguay as a person with no end date in sight. I could only be in Uruguay for a maximum of two years under them because of other financial concerns such as student loans to be paid back. I could have raised that high cost before going back, but again, it's much easier to have people commit to monthly giving because that is a more achievable goal.

There are two particular moments that stick out in my head that helped me to see more clearly that these tools from my mission organization were not set up to be useful to people in my situation. While reading one of the mandatory books on fundraising, I made it through about 180 pages, and I was nearing the end of the book. I took in all the information that the book shared on how to effectively fundraise, and in the last few pages, it addressed the fact that the numerous pages previously written do not apply to all cultures present in the US. While it didn't state it in these exact words, it was written to a primarily white audience. I say this because there were maybe a maximum of 5 pages that were dedicated to alternative options for other ethnic groups such as African American, Latino, or Asian. Literally, just a few paragraphs of that book addressed my actual cultural context when it came to raising funds. It was a bit discouraging in some sense because these were mandatory readings from my mission organization to supposedly help me, but basically everything that I had to read didn't apply to me so it was also a waste of time. This became even clearer because during one of the out of state training sessions on fundraising, a young lady who was of Hispanic origin addressed a similar concern as she had read the same book. She noted how it didn't apply to her cultural context either. What was even more disappointing was the response from one of the people that was giving the training because they didn't have a helpful answer for her concerns. Everything these organizations designed and built to help in fundraising was not created for people like me. It was like saying you will put gas in someone's car for a year but they do not own a vehicle. Sure, it is a nice gift, but it is not very thoughtful or useful because they do not even have a car to utilize. It is like offering to babysit for a friend so that he and his wife can have a date night, but they have not been able to bear children so far in their marriage. It is like giving winter coats to the homeless that live in a tropical climate. The intention may be to help, but it ends up showing a huge disconnect in the mindset of the two sides.

Eventually, I was able to get permission from my mission organization to go back to the mission field and move my life there. I spent 14 months under their banner, and in that time, I learned that I did not really need them. After several months back in Uruguay, I had to really take a step back and ask myself, what was the benefit of being a part of their organization? Ultimately, the real question I had to answer for myself was "Are they doing anything for me that I can't do for myself, and better?" The answer to that question ended up being "no." There was not much communication on a regular basis between me and the home base. Most of my interaction was with the missionaries who were already in the country doing the work like me. Part of this was because they were like my bosses in-country, but really the same things we did in our relationship could have been done without the ties to the mission organization. The mission organization was a place where people could send funds, but beyond that, there was not much that they added. On top of that, they were eating into the relatively low resources that I had coming in to support me for the purposes of their operating costs.

Although they are parachurch organizations, there are aspects that are run like a business as well. There are people who are working in a regular 9 to 5 kind of way. No one is doing these jobs for free, and in order to run the organization, it takes resources and money. Those who are organizing papers, files, accounts, teams, etc. also do so in a full-time manner, and they have to get paid as well. Just like the missionaries in the field, those back home at the base have to make a living. These resources could come from a number of areas. Donors can give to the mission organization as a whole in order to support the work that is being done. Also, people can opt to support an individual missionary and the work that person or family is doing. I mention the business aspect of these organizations because in my experience, any money a missionary might receive is not completely theirs for the work they are doing in the country of their calling. Because there are operating costs, there is a percentage of each donation that is taken that goes towards the operation of the organization.

If mission organizations have anything in common with a regular business, it is that we can look at the missionaries as employees. They are under the banner of that "company" and they are expected to comply with the rules and regulations of that organization by doing what is asked of them. This makes perfect sense in most jobs as someone that is getting paid to do the work should follow the guidelines of the workplace, whatever they may be. While the relationship between a mission organization and the missionaries is very similar to the relationship between an employer and employee, there is one very huge difference that is a part of the missions organizations I have come across - the employees have to generate their own income outside of the actual work they do. In a sense, it is kind of like telling an athlete that he can play professionally. He can be on the team, wear the jersey, and play in the game, but the team is not going to pay him to play. Any of the income he receives comes from whatever outside sponsorships that he gets. The team provides teammates to play with and other teams to play against, but they don't provide much else. Furthermore, because he is officially a part of that team, the team gets a part of the earnings from his sponsorships. I use this analogy to help show the reality of the situation for those who desire to choose this path. Surely, if this same logic applied to the jobs that many of you are working now, you would opt to go another route for your employment. I know this road has worked for many, and there are a great number who have no issue with this arrangement. However considering all of the factors, there is a group of us that does not receive much benefit from this pathway.

Chapter 7: "I can't get no help in here, today."

Let us take a moment to look at what we see being done in the black church. We recognize the need to support people for the work that they do in ministry. In any given church, there are people on payroll. The two positions that come to mind where there is a recognized need for an ongoing financial contribution is in the form of pastors and musicians. At a minimum, it's the pastor. Pastors, in particular, are recognized as having an important role, and it is a role in which they should receive their due pay for the service they provide to the church. They know that the pastor will be involved in the church as a leader and is responsible for the spiritual direction of the church. Musicians in the black church have also carried a weight as participants in the body who receive some form of payment for the services they provide to the church. I want to note that the musician position being a paid role is something that is more unique to black churches as there are a number of white churches that do not pay the musicians who play for their weekly services. Of the differences between the cultures of white and black churches, this is generally one of them. Being an experienced musician, I have to mention that from a logical standpoint, this makes sense. Gospel music in particular is a more advanced style of music compared to the style of music that is played in many white churches. It takes much training to become proficient. That being said, if someone is going to play in a black church, they need to have a particular set of skills that is not common whereas in many white churches, the music that is played is not as demanding. As a result, there is a wider range of people that could potentially participate in the musical arts at any given white church. Again, none of what I say here is 100% across the board, but from my experience in both areas, this is true in the majority of cases.

So why do I mention these examples? It is to point out that those in the black church do recognize the need to support people for their work in the church at some level. It is not a completely foreign concept. I believe the disconnect comes in not categorizing a church's full-time missionary among those who are worthy of ongoing support like those who are in the previously mentioned positions.

First, we must think again about how many black missionaries we know. Do you know anyone who has moved their life to serve the Lord in another country? If the answer is yes, you are already in a small number of people because I would bet that most people would say that they don't know any black missionaries. Sure, they may have seen those who do shorter trips, but the population of full-time black missionaries is quite small. So because we are not seen often or ever, I believe it causes the value of our work to be misplaced.

The way black missionaries are typically treated and supported usually falls under the category of guest preacher. A guest preacher might be invited on any given Sunday. It could be a special day for the church or maybe just a day when the pastor has decided to give another preacher an opportunity to share the word of God that week. They preach their sermon, and many times an extra offering is raised for the guest speaker. This is a moment to show appreciation for the person who brought the preached word to the church that day. It may be an extra sacrificial gift on behalf of those in the congregation, yet it is done out of thanks and support for what that guest preacher has done. Typically, this is the same thing that happens to our black missionaries. If the pastor knows about the missionary visiting their church, he may give them some time to speak about what they have done or will do on the mission field. It might be anywhere between 5-10 minutes which is just enough to give an overview but nothing too detailed. Afterwards, an offering is usually raised to give a boost to the missionary's endeavors.

While these times are greatly appreciated and needed, it can be compared to an end of the year bonus that someone receives at their job. Bonuses are always good and probably help to cover an extra bill that came up. It might even help with something like getting somebody an extra Christmas gift, but what holds more weight than that bonus in the long run is the job that pays that person on a regular basis. While a bonus is good, you won't have enough money to survive the 12 months of the year if you had to depend only on that. If that is someone's only income, they may find themselves quickly on the streets.

Considering all of this, I don't want to imply that pastors, musicians, or any other paid member of the church do these jobs as their only source of income. While there are pastors that are fortunate enough to be full-time in their role, it is much more common in the black church that these leaders have to have a secular job in order to live decently in the city where they are serving. I would like pastors especially to be able to focus on their ministry, but the need for secular work is inevitable many times. Most of our churches just do not have the resources to provide for a pastor in that manner, even though they may have the desire to do so. Therefore, adjustments are made so that all parts of the body can continue to work as smoothly as possible. While the fullness of a pastor's living costs are often not able to be covered by the church, there is still an effort put forth by the members to do what they can to make the pastor's load weigh a bit less.

Why are there churches that have this treatment with the pastor but not necessarily with missionaries if both parties are doing work connected to the church in an ongoing manner? I believe that many times, these churches do not see the work of the missionary as part of what they do. We can bring up the quote, "Out of sight, out of mind." If something is going on thousands of miles away, then it is hard for someone to have that work present in their mind, especially when it is going on in a society that the congregation has no clue about. It could also be that the work outside of the church, or even outside of the city, is just not important to the people of the church. A few might feel like they have more important things going on locally and therefore see it as a waste of resources to contribute to something that has no direct effect on their current context. I want to say this and I want you all to feel the weight of what I am saying with this next sentence - when the church is not aiding in missions near and far, it is missing a very important part of what we are called to do as Christians. To quote Matthew 28:18-20,

"(18) *Then Jesus came to them and said, 'All authority in heaven and on earth has been given to me. (19) Therefore go and make disciples of all nations, baptizing them in the name of the Father and of the Son and of the Holy Spirit, (20) and teaching them to obey everything I have commanded you. And surely I am with you always, to the very end of the age."*

Jesus sent His disciples out to all nations and "all the world" as it is echoed in the last chapter of Mark. Our influence as the Body of Christ needs to be widespread. I do not want my words to be misconstrued so do not believe that I am saying that every church should have a missionary sent out to a foreign land. That is not always realistic. What I am saying is that every church body should have some kind of influence outside of where they are currently stationed. Too many churches stay within their four walls and do not even impact the community in which they are located. That is a bare bones situation. As believers, we should have our influence be felt on many different levels because it is what Jesus called us to do.

I believe that it is hard for some churches to see the need for influence near and far. Because of the history of the black church especially, I have seen that our Christian walk stays within our culture, and it does not live in the fact that we share the same Christ with brothers and sisters in South America. The same God that Christians praise in Russia is that same God that we serve. Those who teach the gospel in Japanese are preaching about the same God that transformed our lives. Our familial network is literally worldwide and understanding this helps us to recognize the importance of mission work and supporting those who are doing the work of God abroad. The connection we have with the family in Christ supersedes nearly every other tie on this earth because it is one that lasts eternally.

I was able to serve God in a better way not just because of Christians stateside that supported me but because I also had Christians in Uruguay that aided me as they could while I was there. It has literally been an international effort, and this is exactly what Jesus called us to do. Imagine that you were dying and never going to see your family again. What would you say to those closest to you? They would probably be the words you deemed most important. You would leave them with words that have a lasting impact. In Jesus' last words, he told his disciples to continue spreading His message to all the ends of the earth.

I want the local church to see that the work of a missionary is not just the work God has called that individual to do. It is the work of the church as a whole. The only difference is the role that each part plays. Everybody cannot go and do what a missionary does. Everyone is not equipped to go and do what they do. The missionaries are playing their part in the call of Christ, and they are an extension of the church. They are the hands and feet that are given agency by the rest of the body. A leg by itself has little use if it is not attached to anything. A leg attached to the body is not functioning fully if it is missing its partner leg. It is hard to write properly if the hand is missing a thumb. The mouth cannot speak clearly with no tongue. I say this because the missionary is just a piece of the body. They are the physical representation of the church that goes to these places, but they cannot operate fully without the rest of the body functioning and supporting it in the way that it was designed to support. It is much easier to run with all of your toes in their proper place, and the missionary can accomplish their goals more easily with the church behind them. I Corinthians 12:25-26 says,

"(25) so that there should be no division in the body, but that its parts should have equal concern for each other. (26) If one part suffers, every part suffers with it; if one part is honored, every part rejoices with it."

The church stateside is a part of the missionary work just as much as the missionary on the field is. When this is understood, I believe there will be a shift in how we, as a whole in the black church, are supporting our missionaries. Although God may call a specific person to go to a distant location, the call to be involved in missions is from God to all of His followers. The only thing that each person has to do is decide which part of that call they are going to be - the goer or the sender.

Chapter 8: My Transition Away From a Mission Organization

Because the money began to run out and I knew that my work in Uruguay had not yet been completed, I began to look for more ways to continue the ministry I was doing. Even while being a part of the mission organization, the funds I was getting monthly were still not enough to cover what I needed in order to maintain a lifestyle in Uruguay without something extra. Before leaving for Uruguay, the mission agency organized a budget for me, and that was the amount that they would send to me on a monthly basis. What I was receiving from donors on a monthly basis did not reach that amount, but the strategy was to combine the one-time gifts and the monthly donations in order to meet the budget we had set for my expenses each month. I was able to be there for 14 months through those combined funds, but as I've explained before, one-time gifts eventually run out. As soon as the money runs out, the ministry has to end.

There was a time that I met with a missionary that I randomly came across in Uruguay. I told him about my predicament about wanting to continue my work there without a mission organization. He mentioned a few different ideas and among them was one that eventually worked better for my situation.

Everyone's situation is a little bit different, and surely the path that I took will not be the best for all black missionaries. In this coming section, I will tell you all what my path was, and hopefully, I will give other black missionaries ideas that will help them on their journey. I will mention this before continuing - as I am still in my time of serving the Lord in foreign lands, I am still not a fully funded missionary. I also have to be aware that this may potentially never be my reality at any point. I am still conscious of the church context from which I come. However, had I implemented the following method earlier, things would have worked more in my favor from the beginning. There were a number of setbacks I had to face as a result of the transition.

The missionary that I spoke with told me about someone he knew that had basically worked out an arrangement with his local church. He spoke with the leaders of the church so that they could set up an account specifically for him so that people could donate to the international work that he was doing. It was not the same as a mission organization, but I must say that I believe this method is how things should be from the beginning. It is closer to the biblical examples of missions that we have. There are a lot of things in the bible that we don't see, and one of them is a mission organization. This is not to say that the end result of what they do is bad or unbiblical. Rather, the root of what we do see being done by mission organizations was done by the church congregations in the Bible. They were the ones that supported the people that were sent out and sent funds to help others in far away places.

"(2) While they were worshiping the Lord and fasting, the Holy Spirit said, 'Set apart for me Barnabas and Saul for the work to

which I have called them.' (3) So after they had fasted and prayed, they placed their hands on them and sent them off." -Acts 13:2-3

The first missionaries that we see being sent out in the Bible are Paul and Barnabas. In their intimate time with God, they received their call from the Holy Spirit and were assigned where to go by God. In this case, we see that God was the one who called the individuals to go and do the work, and it was the church that aided them in this call from God. We see here that they prayed for them and sent them off. We see that they also received financial support from the other churches such as the Philippian church (Phil. 4:15-16). Although they received this monetary support from their churches, they also showed their willingness to support themselves through secular work as we see Acts 18:3, informing us that Paul was a tent-maker. There was no need to have an entity outside of the church for missions because those of the individual congregations were already doing their part to support the work of the Lord.

During my transition, I liked the idea of utilizing my church as the base that sends me out because it still kept things looking official for those who wanted to support. I know that sometimes people are hesitant to send money to a person directly. Others have tax concerns, and if they don't send money through certain avenues then they will be missing out on benefits. Also, there is some level of accountability. If you send funds to an individual's bank account, one could suspect that this person is going to do whatever they please with the money. If it is sent through a church, there is a higher level of faith that these funds will be used for the designated purpose. These are all concerns that I knew donors would have, and I wanted to alleviate these doubts in the best way possible. As a missionary, you want to eliminate as many potential barriers as possible so that people will be more willing to support.

As the local church account path is the direction I ultimately chose, I want to explain some of the things that I did, and more importantly had the ability to do, that are specific to my situation. These opportunities in my journey opened up because of talents and abilities that I had and was able to present as part of my ongoing work. The great thing about the Body of Christ is that we are a diverse people with many different gifts and abilities. Before I explain the path that led me to creating a more reasonable way to collect funds, I want to encourage each black missionary to use their gifts and talents to their advantage. God has equipped us in different ways, and He did it on purpose with each individual. I am an introvert and people don't generally think of introverts as those who go out and minister to people. What they don't realize is that introverts have a different way of connecting with people, and there are times where that is useful. Extroverts have their time and place as well, but that does not mean that the mission field is exclusive to them. Keep this in mind as you are walking in what God has called you to do. He didn't make any mistakes in creating you the way that you are. He gave you interests, talents, and gifts that will be useful to the path He laid out for you.

Upon going back to the US after those initial 14 months, I eventually talked with my pastor and proposed this idea to him. I was no longer going to be a part of the same mission organization because it was not beneficial to my particular path, but God still had more work for me to do in Uruguay. I told him about the idea of having the church open an account specifically for the mission work that I was doing in Uruguay, and I wanted to see if that was something that the church would be willing to do.

I'll stop here and explain this situation in more detail because there are some details that are important. At that point in my life, I had had a relationship with my pastor for 8 years. Before I became a part of his church, we were in seminary together. Through time, an internship, and the guidance of the Lord, I began attending his church, and we have been working together in ministry since then. Even before I formed part of his church, he was an early supporter of my work in Uruguay. Ever since the initial three week trip, he has been there. He has been a pastor and mentor to me for years. Even as I write this, our relationship spans 15 years, and we still have weekly calls to pray and read scripture together. I mention this because I want to recognize it as a factor that everyone may not have present in their situation. Depending on your church, you may have a more distant relationship with your pastor. This particular aspect could vary greatly depending on the situation. However, I still recommend this path if you, as a black missionary, are playing some kind of active role in your church. It may be more difficult for a church to get behind you if they just see you as a pew member. If you have not been an active member of a church, or if you don't have an active relationship with a leader in your church, it could be a tougher hill to climb by going this route. In general, I suspect that the black missionaries reading this are active members of their churches in some capacity. However, we know that being an active member does not negate you from feeling the call to serve the Lord in foreign lands. Above all, I wanted to give this insight to my particular situation so that this aspect can be considered if you too decide to implement this pathway in your fundraising journey.

I mentioned this idea to the pastor because I believed it would be beneficial to the ministry in Uruguay. However, I did not just say that I wanted a bank account for my work and leave it at that. I also made sure to present this idea with everything that was needed to make it work in the long run while adding benefits to the church as well.

This particular church is a smaller church, and the average member is on the latter side of life. I say this because there was an element of technology that had to be implemented in order to have this road be successful. The pastor gave me time with the members of the church to present this idea so that they could approve it or not. So here is what I did - I told the church about the bank account for the mission work and how it would benefit me, but along with it, I brought the opportunity to have a website and the option of online giving for its members and anyone else who wanted to give to the church. As I mentioned, the church has an older population, and there was not much technology implemented in its ministry. The church had no website, and I offered to create and manage the website. This would be a way for the church to have an online presence and be visible to more people. I am a photographer and filmographer also so I could take any of the photos or videos that needed to be added on the website for the time being. Overall, it would be another portal to reach people, and it would open up the option for online giving which turned out to be a tremendously helpful tool in times of COVID which was unforeseen at that time. Through the website, people would be able to give to the church, learn about our ministries, see about the work in Uruguay, and give towards the ongoing efforts.

This is what I decided to present to sweeten the deal. While I believe the church would have and should have supported my proposal without any mention of a website or anything, it did not hurt to have something that they could tangibly see as a benefit as well. I mentioned earlier that people often forget about missionaries because they are not around, but a website is something that you can interact with everyday without much issue. At the base of it, my idea was to present it to them in such a way that it would not make sense to reject my proposal. There were only advantages all around. On top of this, I was not trying to get any special financial commitment from them. I did not ask them to donate money towards my work in Uruguay. My ask was simply that they allow a way for people to give funds through the church in a way that is official, secure, and beneficial to everyone. I will mention that although the church as a whole was not giving towards the work in Uruguay at that time, they later decided to do so as an extra blessing to me. This was never something I asked from them directly, but God moved it upon their hearts to do so.

Again, I mention that I made sure that they did not have to do any work to make this process happen. I did all the work to build the website. I investigated what was needed to connect the website to the online giving for both myself and the church. The main person who had to do any extra steps with me was the pastor as he was the leader and had authority when it came to creating the accounts and everything that was needed to make it all work together. If anyone has ever run their own business, you know that in the beginning stages you have to wear many hats. As I just mentioned, I was the one who built the website, took pictures, arranged the online payment service, and was still responsible for getting the funds from the people. Even though I had to do these different tasks, it still turned out to be a better way for me to operate than being under a mission organization, and it would have helped me immensely to implement this same strategy from the very beginning.

As I said, even today I am not a fully funded missionary, but even with that change from the mission organization to the church, I had a huge advantage. The mission organization I was with took out almost 20% of any funds that I had raised. I already had relatively low support but taking ⅕ of what little I received made things even more difficult. Nothing in this life is free, and although I chose another route and had to arrange a payment service, this newer service only takes 3% of the money donated. That is a huge shift especially when the funds you have to work with are already limited.

Chapter 9: Trials in Resuming the Mission

I recommend a path similar to the one I took from the start for a number of reasons. Most of all, it is wise to do so because having to change your rhythm in the middle of your work can be detrimental to the progress you have made in your mission field. In that first year of living in Uruguay, I feel like I was able to make the most ministerial progress when compared to all the following years. This mainly was because I had more time to dedicate to the work of the Lord. I was not yet working a regular job in Uruguay so basically everything that I did was related to building the kingdom of God. I was able to spend time with the right people and build and nurture relationships at a magnitude that is not quite possible with other preoccupations in life. Being a single man frees me up even more as there is no wife at home to worry about. As it is written in I Corinthians 7:32-33:

"(32) I would like you to be free from concern. An unmarried man is concerned about the Lord's affairs - how he can please the Lord. (33) But a married man is concerned about the affairs of this world - how he can please his wife."

This is not to say that I do not desire to be married, but I recognize that during this period, I have been able to focus more on God's work and devote myself to it in ways that are not afforded to those with other responsibilities. In a similar fashion, not having a regular day job also meant that I could spend time with others who were in a similar position. It made me available to the people in a way that I have not been since that time.

The church gave me a more favorable funding situation, but because I was still not a fully funded missionary, I had also been making plans to work a regular job upon getting back to Uruguay. Being an English teacher had been mentioned to me several times during those first 14 months so I took time during that 6-month reorganization period in the US to equip myself to be an English teacher, and I became a certified English as a foreign language teacher. Upon returning to Uruguay, I had something that I could do to actively take care of my ongoing costs. This is another key recommendation for my black missionaries out there. If you are in a position where you cannot attain fully funded status, use your skill sets to get some kind of work. English is the most widely spoken language in the world and people in non-English speaking countries are often looking to learn. Native English speaking teachers are seen as more valuable because it's their mother tongue so the entry into the field is a bit easier.

The idea behind this is not to have the highest paying job, but rather something to supplement the funds you receive from back home. Neither is the idea to pour all of your time into the secular job in which you find yourself. Do it as part-time as is reasonable. I had to learn this through suffering. I became completely drained in my first year of teaching English because

I was unaware of the load I had signed up to bear. I tried to make sure I had a decent amount of classes to teach because I was unsure of the amount of monthly support I would receive under this new system. At the same time, I did not schedule my work in a way that was beneficial to my ministry. When on the mission field, it is best to schedule your secular work around the work of God and not the other way around, and that is something I discovered the hard way. Ideally, all missionaries would not have the burden of needing to work a secular job, but when necessary, we should do our fair part to make sure that the mission is accomplished. This is part of why I say do enough to supplement the funds that are needed because if you pour all your life and energy into your secular job, you will not be at your best when it's time to do the work of the Lord. The call from God is the main reason you are there, not to work a regular job.

There were other areas of my ministry that took a hit in this time of transition. I wasn't on the field for 6 months, and they happened to be six months during the most important time of the year where a lot of the social activity in the country was happening. Most of the widespread social activity happens during the scholastic year, and during the summer months, things are more on the chill side. During the transition, I also lost supporters. For my initial run, I had a number of people come on board to be monthly givers, but upon changing platforms and thus making people change over to another system, I lost people in the transition. You can send out all the newsletters with the right information, but that still doesn't mean that people are going to bother to change what they already had in place. Some people get comfortable, and if you make them switch platforms in this fashion, it's just like having another lost supporter. Also, the ministry flow that I was in previously had to be rejuvenated. Certain endeavors that I had going on the mission field had to be put on pause. If I was playing a role in a group, that position had to be filled in my absence in order for that group to function in a similar fashion. There were a number of things that I had built in those first 14 months that I had to either reconstruct from the bottom again or just completely leave it behind and do something else in its place upon returning to the country. These are consequences that I had to deal with as a result of not knowing what was my best path from the beginning, and having the right information on the front side would have saved me from unnecessary setbacks and could have even helped to save more souls. I had to learn the hard way, and in part, this is why I have written this book. I do not want others like me to be tripped up by the same obstacles I faced.

III

What Do You Need To Do?

Chapter 10: Move Like a Black Missionary

Since the first purpose of this book is to help other black missionaries such as myself, I want to use this section to specifically address that crowd first. Afterwards, I will address those who are looking to support black missionaries. I recognize that each person's situation may be different so I'll try to keep the most important and relevant information at the forefront while still adding particular details as to what aided me in my journey.

As a black missionary who is deciding to manage their missionary funds without a mission organization, you should find what I will call a "house." This will be the entity that will be your base stateside while you are abroad. This should be a non-profit 501(c)(3) organization. It could be a church or a parachurch organization. My recommendation is to use your home church because you are already part of this body. Depending on the size of the church, the timeline to get things approved and moving could differ. Since the church in my situation is smaller, that means there are less hoops to jump through. There were not multiple boards that I had to talk to in order to get approval. Neither did I have to wait an especially long time. With bigger churches, I imagine things may move a bit more slowly, especially if your presence in the church has not been seen as super important among the leaders. This can be a complicated matter especially if your church is a large church. It is easier to go unnoticed in these situations even if your desire has been to play an active role in one of your church's ministries. Either way, we must note that building rapport and having a positive reputation in your church goes a long way. Unfortunately if that has not been built previously, then the process could take a bit longer for you.

The goal is to have this house through which you can set up an account and allow people to send funds to support you in an ongoing manner. Depending on your situation, you should be ready to do the setup work for them. There may be churches or parachurch organizations that prefer to set things up for you. When you tell them what you need to be able to have support, they may already have people in place that can organize things in this area. If not, be prepared to do it yourself. It may require a process of learning what is needed and how to do it all, but this step is important.

Even if they have the people who can set up everything for you, there is an area of this that you want to be a part of regardless, and that is knowing what funds are coming in and who is giving. There are different ways to accomplish this, but we will talk about it in a little bit. When I was part of a mission organization this was an area that was lacking. The main reason for this was because they happened to be overhauling their system, and for the majority of my active time with them, I had no clue who was giving money and how much I was receiving. I was blind to my finances in that aspect. I would still receive the money every month, but if I wanted to have any other details on my funds, I would have to contact someone directly from the organization. I had no direct access to that information myself. The missionary should be among the first people to know who is giving towards their work. The church or non-profit organization will have to see what you receive as well, and there is not a single issue with that. However, you need to make sure that you have access to not just the donation information but also direct access to whatever bank account is set up for you.

Having a separate account is very important in this case because you don't want your finances to be mixed with the rest of the funds that your house receives. It should be a relatively easy process, but you, the missionary, should be there when this is done because you are the one who will need access to this account, especially when you are on the mission field. Of any name that is attached to that particular account, the missionary has to be among them. Any bank card or other kind of account access that is used needs to be connected in a direct way to the missionary as well. When abroad, you also need to know how you will access your money. This is of the utmost importance. You should know how to get your money from the account and what charges may be attached to you accessing that money.

In my situation in Uruguay, I could use my bank card from the US to pay for things in almost any situation that accepted debit or credit cards. Paying with my US card automatically exchanged the money to the local currency, and there was a very minor charge for the transaction. In some situations, I was even given a discount for using my foreign card. In my particular context, I believe this was done as a way to promote tourism. Either way, it is good to be aware of these details as every country can have its peculiarities. Using my bank card is generally how I paid for things after finding out this information. Still, there were some exceptions as payments dealing directly with the government, like charges for processing my residency, needed to come directly from a Uruguayan currency. I also had the option to withdraw money from ATMs in the local currency if I needed to have cash on hand. This came with its own minor charge for withdrawing money from a foreign account. Another recommendation is to have a bank account that is native to the country in which you will be serving. This will be most beneficial if you have a regular job in your country, but it could also have other benefits like being able to transfer money more easily to and from people who live there. The benefits and pathway to having a local bank account may differ greatly depending on what country you are in so I won't speak in too much detail about it. However if it is possible to do so, I recommend that you have a local bank account in your country of ministry.

After figuring out what entity will be your house, you need to find a way for people to be able to send you funds. The first part to arrange is the electronic giving because that is the easiest way to set up recurring payments. While there are a number of platforms that can be used, the particular one I use is called Givelify. It is a platform specifically designed for churches and parachurch organizations so that they can have an avenue for electronic giving. A number of churches that I know use it, and it has been a good option for me. Furthermore, it allows administrators of the Givelify account to view their giving and create different envelopes for those that want to support specific areas of the mission. It helps to organize the funds and manage finances a little better. As I briefly mentioned before, no one should expect any service like this to be free so the company takes about 3% of every donation. Considering the alternatives, I would say that is very reasonable. Each person should find the service that works best for them in this area, but here, I have presented an option that has worked for me and others.

Everyone is not technologically inclined, and there are others who are not willing to give online. Therefore, you should also create an avenue for people to be able to give in a physical manner as well. If you are attached to the church, it would be best to have an arrangement where people can send money to a church address and have donations marked specifically to go towards your mission endeavors. Those that handle the funds of the church would then be able to deposit the money into your account so that you can later have access to it. If this is not a viable option, then alternatively, you could have donors send the money or check to a trusted family member or friend so that they can deposit the money to the correct place. The idea in all of this is to have as few steps as possible while at the same time making the process convenient for everyone. Our path in fundraising is already hard so the need for carving out a smooth road so that others can join us on the journey is often part of the process.

Chapter 11: Asking - a Necessity

After getting things set up with your house and having the account ready to receive donations, we still need to do the next part which still requires a significant amount of effort - letting people know that you need funds to carry out God's work in another country. I say this meaning that you need to actually inform people about your plans and ask them for money to support you. Either way you look at it, this is an essential part of the journey. People will not know what to give to you if they don't know about what you're doing. They won't know you need money from them if you don't ask for it. It's like the scripture says in Romans 10:14-15:

"(14) How, then, can they call on the one they have not believed in? And how can they believe in the one of whom they have not heard? And how can they hear without someone preaching to them? (15) And how can anyone preach unless they are sent? As it is written: 'How beautiful are the feet of those who bring good news!'"

We, as Christians, have the responsibility to inform those who don't know about the good news of Jesus Christ. It is essential information for non-believers because it can transform their lives. Many people do not follow Christ simply because they have not heard of Him, and that is why His people carry such a huge responsibility to share the Word with everyone they can. In a similar fashion, some people in our churches are not supporting our missionaries simply because they don't know about the work they are doing. Upon hearing about how God is moving in the life of the missionary, these believers may be moved to join that work as senders. Oftentimes, the key is just to make sure they are informed, and God will take care of the rest.

Although this book may have seemed to focus on some negative things that I experienced while being part of a mission organization, it wasn't all bad. Like I mentioned, they did provide tools and training to help us in our fundraising process. Among these items were kits that helped us with our correspondence. We had pictures with the emblems and logos of the organization presented in a way that made us look official. When sending out correspondence, we could attach these items to make our operation look more appealing. These are good additions, and I believe they should be applied when dealing with your audience. It takes a bit of extra effort, but it also adds to how you are perceived. It shows that you are taking things seriously, and it is not a lazy operation. These images can be developed by someone more professional, but with the mindset of being as financially conscious as possible, it's good to do as much as you can yourself. The point is that you want to do as much as you can to let your network know that you are serious about what God has called you to do, and that even carries over to your branding as a missionary.

Network

In this kind of fundraising, your network is key. During

my early years, getting linked to a variety of churches helped me to move closer to reaching my goal. I worked with my pastor to get in touch with other churches in our network. Again, I want to emphasize that having pastoral support in this area can be a huge advantage for you not just within your church, but also when it comes to having influence with other congregations. My pastor was able to connect me with the pastors of other congregations in order to arrange a time in which I would be able to go and share what I was doing and ultimately, see what kind of support I could get. Because most of these opportunities to share my international work would usually come on a Sunday, that means I would have to miss out participating in my own church service some weeks. If you play a noticeable role in the church most Sundays then you should inform your team and leadership about your plans so that things can continue to move forward smoothly.

One of the reasons that mission organizations emphasize full-time fundraising is because it can be an exhausting task. The idea is to utilize every opportunity to gain monthly supporters. I say this because although I was not afforded the chance to fundraise in a full-time manner, there were some days where I had to put in extra hours to reach the necessary crowds. For example, there are churches that have multiple services. A single church could potentially have a bible study on Wednesday evening, a service on Saturday evening, and two services on Sunday morning. If given the opportunity to speak at each of those gatherings in a single week, it is a good idea to attend each one. That could be an exhausting experience when considering your other responsibilities in life, but it pushes you closer to the goal. You never know who can be in those crowds that will end up supporting you in a major way.

For these speaking opportunities, it is also good to have your pitch prepared for different scenarios. The usual amount of time given for the missionary to speak is between 5-10 minutes. However, there have been times when I have been given a whole bible study period to speak to a group about what God is and has been doing through me in Uruguay. It is good to be ready for each of these situations at any given moment because there were times when I went to a church thinking I would just be the appetizer, but I ended up being the entrée. Therefore, I had to make adjustments on the fly. Plan ahead in case your situation changes unexpectedly. If you go prepared with slides and a visual presentation, it helps make your work come alive to your audience and fill up extra time if needed. If the church does not have the capability for that, opening up a time for questions and answers is a good way to respond to any inquiries the people might have as well as utilize the time that you have with them. Many times, going to the mission field includes a whole world that is completely foreign to the average person. It is impossible to inform a crowd of all the details during a general presentation so receiving questions helps to answer the specific things that are on people's minds.

In each speaking opportunity as a black missionary, you need to be as clear and transparent as possible when talking about the realities of your situation. The things I previously covered in this book need to be covered in some form when you speak to the people. It is imperative to state that the goal is not just a one-time donation but ongoing, monthly support. Your mission work is not a short-term endeavor. Please do not understate the importance of one-time giving as that is an essential part of your funding. We do, in fact, have one-time costs that require an extra push. Many times, the airfare, initial rent deposit, buying household supplies and furniture are things that we need in order to get established in our new country. The setup costs can be one of the biggest hurdles to get over when moving abroad. Still, the ongoing support sustains the mission for the duration of our time in that land.

If nothing else, make this the point of what you say, but also connect it to the work that you are doing. In whatever ministry you are doing internationally, make it real to those that are sending you. If you are planting a church, you can compare it to the care that an actual plant needs to grow. You don't just put the seed in the ground and water it once, hoping it becomes a thriving plant afterwards. You do the initial work, but as it continues to grow, you continue to water it. You have to make sure it gets the right amount of sunlight. You have to make sure you don't overwater it. There are different stages that require different kinds of care in an ongoing manner. In the same way, senders should be with the goers through the different stages of their ministry because the missionary will have to adapt with life and their ministry as it develops.

It Takes a Village

To make this more clear, I want to give an example that came from my time in Uruguay. During my initial three week trip, some members of my group spoke with a young man about Christ. He listened to them, but did not make a decision for Christ at that moment and continued to live his life as before. The following year, another group of missionaries happened to come across this young man and share the truth of the gospel with him. He found it interesting that two separate groups spoke to him about a similar thing. Even after speaking with these missionaries the following year, he still did not move towards Christ. However, he noted the strangeness of these occurrences. He may not have been aware of it in its fullness at the time, but God was obviously reaching out to him. A year after this second encounter, he came across some Uruguayan Christians and began to form a relationship with them. Through this third encounter, he was able to have his eyes opened to the truth of the Lord and finally made a decision to follow Christ. It didn't just happen because of that first group, but God continuously used people through the years to draw in this young man. This is one of the main reasons that I decided to continue returning to Uruguay. I knew that in many cases, three weeks would not be enough to cultivate a visible change, especially because of the spiritual climate of the country. God's plan was to nurture this seed that was planted in 2011, and two years later there was fruit seen. This is why we have missionaries in these places to continuously work with those who need this kind of nurturing through the years.

The church should be made aware that the missionary was not designed to be alone in the ministry that they do. It always requires a team that works together. Jesus did not work alone either. Rather, He showed us the importance of having others around us that aid in doing the work of the Kingdom of God. The person that goes is the missionary, but those that send are also an inseparable part of the mission work. Each congregation needs to realize the importance of the role that they play although they are not physically there with you. As we have talked about previously, many black churches simply have not been made aware of how they have handled the area of foreign missions, and we can help by showing them what areas need to be rectified. It is a hindrance to not speak about these things, yet it is important to do it with love and point towards the biblical models that we have. It would also be wise to speak with the pastors of these different congregations about your need for ongoing support because that is what you are ultimately seeking. While it is a possibility that the church as a whole may not commit to supporting you, it is often the individuals of a congregation that step out on faith to support us black missionaries.

There was a black missionary that my mother came across as a married woman in her early 30's. He was a young man who had recently finished college and was looking to dedicate his life to missions in foreign lands. This missionary came to her church and spoke about the work that he was doing. Like many in his position, he was also looking for financial support. He spoke during his allotted time during the service and mentioned that he would be around after the service if anyone wanted to get more information and possibly support. My mother, upon hearing this, was impressed by the young man because when she finished college, dedicating her life to something like this was nowhere close to her thoughts. It was impressive to see someone who was taking that leap of faith. After the service, the missionary was standing around, and not a single person was talking to him. My mother saw him and felt bad because he was embarking on a very brave and important journey, but he received no visible interest from anyone in the church. She approached him and mentioned that she and my father might be able to support him monthly, although it would be a very small contribution. They were not in the best economic position at the time. However, they ended up committing to give him $5 every month. It may seem like a small amount, and the reality is, I don't know how that particular missionary felt about those monthly $5. I can tell you from experience that those $5 every month are more important to the missionary than you might realize. They are important because it shows that you believe in the work that they are doing. It shows that you stand with the missionary. At the end of the day, those monthly $5 could be the difference in someone having the opportunity to hear the word of God or not. I cannot explain to you all the number of ways an extra push like that can change the work that we do as missionaries. As time went on and their financial situation improved, my parents were able to give more, but that initial commitment is what started a ministerial relationship that carried on for many years, and it helped change many lives.

Prayer Power

While we should recognize that the majority of the people you come across will not be financial supporters of your ministry, a part that everyone can participate in is the area of prayer. The reality is that this portion comes before any other part of the process of fundraising. Prayers will pave the way for God's work to be done. We pray to ask God for the provision, but we also pray for those that are going to be our supporters. Still, we need those back home to be praying for us as well. A good way to have your international ministry constantly uplifted in prayer is by keeping people informed through correspondence. My assumption is that sending physical mail from whatever country you are in will not be very efficient. Therefore, many missionaries opt to keep their supporters informed through email. If you have some manner to have physical mail be sent to those who don't use email, it would be a great idea to implement that. Even if people do not decide to support you financially, getting their emails or physical addresses so that they can receive your regular updates is key. This will be your main way of staying connected with those back home while you are on the mission field. During these church visits, you should have an efficient way to collect their information so that they can be added to your list. The primary intent of this is to inform those back home of your international work and let them know how they can be praying for you.

Another purpose of the email communication is that it gives future opportunities for people to become financial supporters of your mission. There are a number of factors that could influence someone's movement in giving. There have been some who started to give in my early years that stopped later on. Others did not give at the beginning, but years later, they decided to become monthly supporters. In part, this was because I had some form of update that I was sending out to them. In your updates, you want to show how God is moving, but you also want to present these people with the opportunity to give financially toward your mission as well. Always leave that door open for the people so that God can use the senders as He pleases. However, the most important part of this email piece is prayer because when you have the right people praying for you, the finances will come.

In the whole fundraising process, keep in mind that often someone that you expected to give might not donate anything while an unexpected person could be a major contributor. I have seen situations where a complete stranger has donated a large amount or committed to monthly giving while someone who has been a close friend of a missionary has given nothing. Fundraising is a strange thing in that way, but God will use who He wants during this process. It is worth knowing that those who give will receive their blessing in return. In this thought, I want to share with the missionaries the importance of praying for those who are supporting you in prayer and in finances. These people are the pillars of your work and are even subject to attacks from the enemy for the same reasons that missionaries are. Pray for them in a way that they will be blessed many times over for the manner in which they have contributed to the work we do as missionaries. My prayer is always that their gifts to my international ministry might appear minuscule in comparison to what God will give them in return for their role in the work.

Coming back home for visits is an essential part of our journey as well although we are dedicating the majority of our time to foreign lands. This has many benefits for us as it can be a time of rest, rejuvenation, and reconnection with those that we left behind. I mention it here in this particular section because it is a good idea to utilize these visits to go see those that have been supporting you. Depending on the funding that you have available, your options may be limited. Visiting these people or churches can be costly depending on where you are located in relation to your supporters. These visits are important to you in a sense that it could be another opportunity to gain more support in prayer and finances, but mainly, it is good just for the people to see you. It shows you that God has kept you in this time, and you can give a report about what has happened on your mission field in a more tangible way. While I know you want everyone to read your emails and correspondence that you send out, that's not going to be the reality of things. However, people are more likely to pay attention to what you are doing when you are right in front of them. It helps on another level when they can see how the funds you have been given have been utilized to build the kingdom of God. These times are the best to be open and honest with the people about the good and the bad. For example, my life has been in danger more than once on the mission field in a very real way. Showing up in person shows them that God has protected you, but you can also make them aware that there are difficulties that come from the work.

There are many challenges that one faces on the mission field as a missionary, and a substantial amount of these are a result of spiritual attacks. This particular subject in its more complete form is a topic for another book, but as I stated before, missionaries are going to a place where there is a spiritual need that they are going to help fulfill. Because we are international workers for Christ, the devil is not going to let God's people work without any opposition, and that can manifest itself in many ways. I would not say that Uruguay is an impoverished nation. While it is lacking in certain areas, you can still find many things there that people in the states have. TVs, internet, malls, transportation, and other modern amenities are all present, yet it is the most secular nation in the western hemisphere with a less than 3% Christian population. The greatest poverty there is of a spiritual nature, and that is why I was called to that land. Even as I prepare to move to Barcelona to carry on more work there, many people may think, "I need to go there for vacation." While it is a popular tourist destination, they have a very similar spiritual situation. Other missionaries are building orphanages in impoverished parts of the world. Still, others are doctors in places that don't have good medical care. Every one of these missionaries is playing an important role, and I say this because I want everyone who reads this to know that their work cannot be done without the support of God's people behind them.

Chapter 12: Support Beams

For those who are senders, my prayer is that you have gained an insight into some of the challenges that we face as black missionaries. While reading about what a black missionary should be doing in their fundraising, some of you may have even imagined some of the things you should do to make their journey easier, and that is the perfect response. More than anything, I desire that you aid them in their journey and help to lift some of the burden that they have to carry. I didn't talk about it too deeply in this book because the topic of this focuses more on finances, but I do want you to realize that there are a plethora of challenges that are faced on the mission field. I am one man, and I can only speak directly from my experiences. However, I know that there is a special kind of spiritual opposition that missionaries face in whatever their arena is. All should do whatever they can to make their burden easier as the work alone can be cumbersome. As I mentioned earlier in the book, it is hard to treat the needs of people if you yourself are not in a position to serve them. It is hard to invite people into your home for bible study if the only living space that you can afford barely has enough room for you. Having financial support from those back home is not about living a luxurious lifestyle. Instead, it is about being able to create more opportunities and spaces to minister to the people of that foreign land.

As supporters, I want you to take a very literal look at what that name is describing. You are the support beams that help the work abroad continue to exist. If you look at any building, it is able to stand because there are columns and supporting structures in place. When crews want to demolish or implode a building, they strategically aim to destroy the effectiveness of those support beams. From the story of Samson, we even see that he targeted just two pillars that were supporting the house where they were. Just by taking out two pillars, everything around him came down. I state this so that you can see the importance of your role. A missionary without supporters will not be able to stand or build anything that stands for very long. So what do you need to do? I'm glad you asked.

Give Space

First, give missionaries space in your church beyond the occasional 5-10 minutes when they are fundraising. I say give them space in the sense that they should be present among the ministries that are named in your church. They should have a space on the same level as ushers, youth ministry, outreach in the community, and musical worship. If your church does not have a mission ministry, then one should be created. Again, this does not mean that someone from the church has to be a full-time missionary. Rather, this promotes the church's involvement in international missions. For most of the black churches that have supported me throughout my journey, I believe that I am the only full-time missionary that they have supported, and that is fine. However in an ideal scenario, most of these churches would be ongoing supporters of my international work if they have no other connection to missions abroad.

We are going to look at an example to see why support from congregations as a whole can be effective on a larger scale. Let's just say that I have had 10 different churches that support my mission. In this, I mean that they have allowed me to speak to their congregation, and they have collected an offering for me as is typical in these situations. If those 10 churches decide to support with just $100 a month, that would cover the before proposed hypothetical need of $1000 a month to be able to operate in a foreign land. When considering this approach, the goal seems a lot easier, especially when considering the amount of people that could potentially be in each church. In theory, it only takes 20 people from each church to give $5 a month toward the missionary fund, and that would cover this amount. Again, this is just an example, but I want to help my people see that it is not a huge stretch to support a missionary in a great way when we band together. I use this amount as an example because it is a nice round number, but depending on their circumstance a missionary could need more. Other countries could have a higher cost of living, or they just might have more members of their family to take care of. The key is to band together in this respect because working together helps make the load easier for everyone.

Giving them a space also helps the missionaries to have a voice. While your church may not be sending anyone out directly, it is essential to open your doors to those who want to speak and are looking for support. Admittedly, this is an area that most churches do fairly well. I have not seen much issue in missionaries not being able to speak about their work at a given church for those 5-10 minutes. It is always a huge help.

However, my special advice to pastors and leaders is to echo and affirm what the missionary is doing as well as the need for their ongoing support. I do not want this to just be about words, but the actions are what truly hold weight. I want to reemphasize that many times, people you thought would support do not end up supporting, but strangers and unexpected people are often the ones who lift us up on this journey. Personally, I have heard a number of times from a pastor that the church as a whole will be supporting my endeavors on a regular basis. After the offering was raised on that day, I didn't receive anything else from the church as a whole. While other individuals stepped up, it should be the pastor and the leaders of the church that are implementing this kind of support in the lifestyle of the church and leading with their example. I mention this in this section because missionaries should not be their only advocates. I am fortunate that in my house, I've had an advocate and people that support me financially and pray for me, but I recognize that this kind of behavior is not present across the board.

Give Prayer

The next thing that you as a supporter should do is pray for your missionaries. As I have said before, this really should be the first thing applied. For the churches that have organized a mission ministry, it would be a good idea to have a team that is in prayer for that missionary in a special way. They should have a particular line of communication where the missionary can communicate with this team directly so that these prayer warriors can be in prayer for them. Aside from this team, the individual supporters should be praying for the missionary. If you know of one, keep them in your prayers. Being on their newsletter list allows you to be informed, and that will help you to know how to pray for them. Take the opportunity to be on that list at a minimum so that your prayers can be more specific for that person. Along with this, I will add that it is important to read the correspondence when it gets to you, whether it is through mail or email. It contains carefully crafted information. I know for a fact that these updates omit many details, but each missionary tries to make it as concise as possible so that the supporters are getting the most relevant information. If you are afforded the opportunity to respond to the emails, you should also do so occasionally. It helps you to connect with those who are abroad. Even writing a short message from time to time telling the missionary that you are praying for them can be a great boost to their morale. I say this from experience, and I am grateful to those who have let me know they are praying for me. Every missionary will not have the luxury of receiving responses in such an open manner. There are some who have to send out coded correspondence because of the censorship and limitations of their country. Either way, keep each missionary you know in your prayers and communicate with them when it's possible. You are often a much needed link to those back home.

Give

The last thing I will say towards what you can do as a sender is to simply give. Give to the work that a missionary is doing and give according to how God has blessed you. Give on a regular basis. Perhaps you cannot do it every month, but maybe a quarterly donation is reasonable for you. Just as missionary visits help the congregations see how God is working across the world in a tangible way, that financial support also helps the missionary see that their church family is with them in a tangible way. The missionary is giving in their own way as well. They are leaving behind a life they've known for something unfamiliar for the sake of winning souls for Christ. This may not be everyone's situation but for me, being a missionary was the very last thing that I wanted to do as a Christian. I would have done anything else in the Body of Christ before being a missionary. Still, when I saw that this was God's will for me, I decided to be obedient because His will supersedes mine, and His plans are greater than mine. My desire is that the Body of Christ, and especially the black church, steps out on that same kind of faith and makes an effort to be more effective in worldwide ministry.

I have said that I am not a fully funded missionary, and that means that I've been working a regular job while still trying to minister to the people. Although there can be opportunities for outreach in that workplace, it can become an obstacle as well, especially if it is not tied to the work that God has called that missionary to do. I made most of my advancements during the time that I was free to focus on ministry opportunities, and as I transitioned into working a regular job to help support the ongoing ministry work, I lost a lot of the momentum that I had and truthfully, never got it back fully. A person can work a 9-5 anywhere in the world. In these cases, God is not calling us to be a manager at a bank or be a waiter at a restaurant. He has called us to minister to these people in these places and more, and we simply need the support of the Body of Christ to help us accomplish this task in a more effective way.

It is hard to go to the mission field solely by one's own work. It is hard for one person alone to maintain the living expenses of a missionary and still be effective in their country of ministry. However, the overall job is made easier when there are many of us working together to do our part. I can move a sofa from one room to the next, but I might risk damage to my body as well as damage to the sofa. It is easier to move it if my brother helps me. Even still, it is easier to move that same sofa if we call a couple of friends to help us move it together. The weight of this work only seems heavy when there are few of us that are working towards the goal. When we band together and each person does their part, what seemed difficult is made easy. My prayer and desire is to see the Body of Christ operate in its fullness, walking rightly in all of the areas in which God has called us to be fruitful.

To Further Support the Author and the Continued Mission Work

Mission Website and Newsletter Sign Up:
https://carvermission.com/

Donate Electronically to Carver's Mission Work:
https://giv.li/kpqnra

Carver's "House" Website:
https://ncccog.org/

About the Author

Carver Scott is a missionary and cultural bridge-builder originally from Columbus, Ohio. He earned his Master of Divinity in Pastoral Leadership from Cincinnati Christian University in 2014 and holds a Bachelor of Arts in Spanish from the University of Cincinnati (2010).

Since 2011, Carver has been serving in missions with a focus on Spanish-speaking communities, dedicating eight full years of work to the people of Uruguay. His ministry has uniquely combined the power of music and cultural connection to communicate the gospel in meaningful and accessible ways. Carver enjoys playing video games, playing hockey, skating, composing and producing music, and watching movies in his free time. *Tales of an African American Missionary: Part 1 - Fundraising* is his first book, and it was inspired by one of the many trials that he has faced as a missionary abroad.

Carver is now preparing for long-term mission work in

Spain, where he will continue reaching and equipping Spanish-speaking populations for Christ. One of his central passions is to empower African American Christians to walk fully in their God-given calling—especially in the realm of global missions, where their voices and gifts are deeply needed.

Subscribe to my newsletter:

✉ https://carvermission.com